Supernatural

Is

Natural

The Blessings of Hearing the Voice of God

Dr. Rick Kurnow

ISBN- 978-0-615-52238-8

Dedication

To my precious wife Dottie who has walked with
me on this amazing journey through the supernatural.
The manifest presence of God has carried us through our many
years of ministry and marriage and has drawn us closer to our Lord
and Saviour Yeshua Ha Mashiach (Jesus The Messiah).

Thank You Lord for speaking to me about writing this book and
filling me with Your Spirit as the words poured from Your heart to
mine. You are Awesome!! I Love You!

Acknowledgements

Many thanks to my dad, Mel Kurnow who helped me edit this
manuscript.. I have much love and admiration for his many years
as a dedicated teacher mentoring and shaping young lives through
English, Journalism and Drama. Also I would like to thank
Rebecca Daugherty, Annette Ettinger and Susan Ozols for their
contribution to the editing process of this book. God Bless you all!

Listen to His Voice

Walk with Me and listen to My voice. I will instruct you in the way that you should go. Trust Me for I know the plans I have for you. Plans to prosper and bless you. Plans to release you from all that tries to bind you. I will in this hour show forth my glory and all the earth will see it.

Many walk in blindness but I will reveal myself in this generation. The wicked will not prevail but I will show my great love to a hurting and maimed people. I will instruct you in the way you should go and I will make your feet like hinds feet in high places.

Look up for your redemption draws nigh. My Word will shine bright in the darkness and I will bring solution to every problem. Rejoice for in this hour I am releasing a great move of my Spirit and the church will arise in power. I am calling forth my bride and I will adorn her. I will give her beauty for ashes and the oil of joy for mourning and the garment of praise in exchange for the spirit of heaviness. I will comfort her in this hour of uncertainty in this world. For I will certainly take care of all that is mine and not one minute detail will be overlooked for I know all things and hold all things in my hands. I AM the Lord your God and I fail not.

Word of the Lord received September 6, 2010

Table of Contents

Introduction ~ So many Voices..iii

Chapter 1 ~ My Journey Begins..............................1

Chapter 2 ~ Genuine or Counterfeit..................................11

Chapter 3 ~God Cares About The Little Things........15

Chapter 4 ~ Dreams & Visions................................21

Chapter 5 ~You Want Me To Give What?.....................27

Chapter 6 ~ The Best Counselor....................................31

Chapter 7 ~Ask Jesus First.......................................37

Chapter 8 ~ Open My Eyes..41

Chapter 9~ Participating in Answered Prayer...................45

Chapter 10~ Saved From Death.............................53

Chapter 11~ Learn To Wait On The Lord...................59

Chapter 12 ~ Get The Picture?..................................65

All scripture quotations are from the New King James Version unless otherwise noted

Supernatural Is Natural

Introduction – So Many Voices

There are so many voices in this world. So how do you know and hear the voice of God? The voice you are hearing could be just yourself and your reasoning, or maybe it could be another person's reasoning. It could very possibly be a deceiving voice from an evil influence like a demonic spirit or satan himself. So how can you be sure you are hearing the voice of God and not the voice of a stranger?

Jesus said in John 10:1-5 *"Most assuredly, I say to you, he who does not enter the sheepfold by the door, but climbs up some other way, the same is a thief and a robber.2 But he who enters by the door is the shepherd of the sheep.3 To him the doorkeeper opens, and the sheep hear his voice; and he calls his own sheep by name and leads them out.4 And when he brings out his own sheep, he goes before them; and the sheep follow him, for they know his voice.5 Yet they will by no means follow a stranger, but will flee from him, for they do not know the voice of strangers."*

He also said in John 10:27 *"My sheep hear My voice, and I know them, and they follow Me."*

God wants you to know Him and for you to know His voice.

If we want to get to know someone, then the more you spend time with them the more you know them. You know what they like, you know the desires of their heart. You learn about their character and as time goes on you get closer and closer. If you were in the middle of a crowd and that person called out your name you wouldn't have to see them to know it was them even though you are surrounded by many voices.

That is the way it is with God. There are so many voices in this world. But it is possible to know God and to know His voice. ***The supernatural is actually very natural for those who learn to know the voice of God.*** Join me on this journey as I share personal experiences that taught me how to hear and recognize the voice of God.

5 Trust in the LORD with all your heart, And lean not on your own understanding; 6 In all your ways acknowledge Him, And He shall direct your paths Proverbs 3:5-6

Rick Kurnow age 13

Chapter 1

My Journey Begins

"I will give you a new heart and put a new spirit within you;
I will take the heart of stone out of your flesh and give you a
heart of flesh.27 I will put My Spirit within you and cause
you to walk in My statutes, and you will keep My judgments
and do them." Ezekiel 36:26-27

My journey began with my growing up in a Conservative
Jewish home with loving parents. Our family would go to the
Synagogue on Saturdays and we would celebrate all the
Jewish holidays. When I was in 2nd grade, I began to go to
Hebrew school after public school to learn how to read
Hebrew and to prepare for my Bar Mitvah. I learned how to
wear the Tallit (prayer shawl) and even how to wear and use
the Tefillin. The Tefillin are small boxes containing scripture
that Jewish people bind on their forehead and arm.

Even though I was learning a lot about my heritage and
religion I did not know God. In fact the miracles I was
learning about in the Tenach (the Hebrew scriptures) I really
didn't believe. On Sundays our synagogue would have
religious instruction classes. I remember the teacher telling
us about the miracle of the parting of the Red Sea. Then she
asked. "How many of you believe that God performed a
miracle?' Some raised their hands. Then she asked "How
many of you do not really believe it was a miracle?" I raised
my hand along with some others so she decided to break us
up into two groups and gave us the opportunity to come up

with our reasons for what we believed. I was the ringleader of my group. We came up with so many reasons as to why this all happened by natural means and not supernaturally. We didn't argue that it didn't happen; we just reasoned it away by scientific natural reasoning.

I studied diligently in Hebrew School to prepare for my Bar Mitvah. I memorized the portion of the Hebrew scripture I was to read on that day. The day was very special for several reasons. Our congregation had built a new synagogue and I was the first to have a Bar Mitvah in the new building. The Cantor (the one who sings the scripture in the synagogue) sang a duet with me during the service and everyone began to cry. The people said that when I got older I should become a Cantor. Little did everyone know that one day I would fulfill that destiny but in a way no one ever imagined.

Oy, my Son The Actor

During this season of my life I decided I wanted to become an actor. I could sing and act and my Dad was a High School teacher who taught English Literature, Journalism and Drama. He got me involved with The Children's Theatre of the Minneapolis Institute of Arts. He was able to get me a professional part at the Tyrone Guthrie Theatre located in Minneapolis. I had an agent and I landed a lead part in a Christmas special on CBS. The night CBS aired the special, I starred in an operetta "Amahl and The Night Visitors," I was Amahl. The story was about a crippled boy who was visited by The Three Kings on their way to find the child that was born to be a king. Amahl wanted to give something, but the only thing he had was his crutches. He sent his crutches with the kings to this Savior King and was healed. Little did I know that the seed from this production was preparing me to meet my Messiah.

It wasn't too long after my Bar Mitvah that my family decided to move to Hawaii. In Hawaii I began acting in the Honolulu Theatre for the Youth. My agent got me some extra parts with Hawaii 5-O and I was interviewed for a major part in a show with Brian Keith called "The Little People," but God had different plans for me.

From Pakalolo to the Bible

I was involved with the competitive speech team at my High School in the storytelling category. I had to come up with a story and then act it out while I told it. So one day I smoked some pakalolo (which is Hawaiian for marijuana) thinking it would make me creative. I chose the book "Where the Wild Things Are" by Maurice Sendak and created a script in a way I could act it out. My speech teacher said it was brilliant and I began to use it in tournaments.

I had a Japanese friend named Mark who was my running partner on the cross country running team and also was involved in competitive speech. He was a spirit filled Christian. He was very smart and everyone in the school liked him. He was different from everyone else but everyone respected him.

One day I asked him if he would like to smoke some pakalolo with me. He said "No. I have something better." "You do? What is it?" I said with expectation thinking it was some sort of drug I could experience. He said " I have Jesus!" I told him I didn't believe in Jesus because I was Jewish. He told me Jesus was Jewish. I exclaimed "No He was not- He was a Christian" Mark then explained to me that Jesus was Jewish and if I would read the New

Testament I would discover how Jewish Jesus really was. So I decided I would read the New Testament. But I didn't.

Not too long after that there was a statewide speech tournament on the Island of Maui with several High Schools competing. Our team flew over to Maui and stayed in a house on the beach in Kihei. The first night we all decided to go sleep on the beach. Mark was reading a Bible devotional and I grabbed it out of his hands and tried to read it. It didn't make any sense to me so I got in my sleeping bag and for the first time I can remember the presence of God came upon me. I recognize it now as the presence of Ruach Ha Kodesh (The Holy Spirit).

As I looked up into the vast stars with the sound of the ocean crashing and the palm trees swaying, something inside of me was reaching out with mind boggling questions that I couldn't reason or figure out. I was asking inside, "Why am I here?" What if there was no such thing as the earth or the universe what would there be? What if there was no such thing as people? I just couldn't figure it out so I decided to pray and ask God somewhere out there. I prayed a selfish prayer that God was about to use to change my life. I prayed, "God if You are really real – I want to get first place in the speech tournament." The following 2 days as I competed God was at work. The awards were held in a huge ballroom at a hotel. When it came to my category they announced "First place Story telling – Rick Kurnow." I was stunned. The crowd jumped to their feet and everyone shouted and cheered as I walked from the back of the ballroom through the crowd. It felt surreal – I felt like I was in a dream. I got my trophy and when I got to the back of the ballroom I said to Mark "I think God did this for me." He said "You can be sure of that" Then he challenged me. He said when I got back to Oahu that I needed to get a Bible and read it. I said I would. And I did.

Is that really God?

" You believe that there is one God. You do well. Even the demons believe -- and tremble!" James 2:19

Now I believed that God was real but I still didn't know Him. My mind began to try to figure God out. One day I had what I thought was a great revelation. I couldn't wait to go tell my friend Mark. As I thought about the pattern of the stars in the sky and now believed God had created it all , I decided that God gave us astrology so we could lead our lives. Wow, think about it, God cared so much for us that He saw to it that there would be a pattern in the universe that would help us every day to lead our lives.

I went to see my friend Mark to tell him about what I figured out. He immediately took me to the Bible and showed me:

Isaiah 47:12-14 "Stand now with your enchantments And the multitude of your sorceries, In which you have labored from your youth -- Perhaps you will be able to profit, Perhaps you will prevail. 13 You are wearied in the multitude of your counsels; Let now the astrologers, the stargazers, And the monthly prognosticators Stand up and save you From what shall come upon you. 14 Behold, they shall be as stubble, The fire shall burn them; They shall not deliver themselves From the power of the flame; It shall not be a coal to be warmed by, Nor a fire to sit before!

He explained that astrology was not from God and that there were many counterfeits for the genuine. He explained that God had a better way of leading us and that was by His Holy Spirit and the Word of God as written in the Bible.

5

I was surprised that I was wrong. It seemed like I had received such a great revelation. So I began to read the Bible. I decided to read the New Testament to see what it had to say. To my surprise I discovered that Jesus was very Jewish. As I continued to read I began to realize that not only was Jesus the Messiah for all people but that He was God. This didn't make sense to me but deep down inside I knew what I was reading was true. I kept trying to figure out God and would come up with some wild ideas. No wonder there are so many religions in this world. People try to understand God from their finite position

From Deception to Delight

"But the natural man does not receive the things of the Spirit of God, for they are foolishness to him; nor can he know them, because they are spiritually discerned." 1 Corinthians 2:14

One day I was sharing with Mark some of my "great ideas" I could tell that he was getting frustrated with me. Finally he said to me "Rick are you saved?" I said "Saved? Whats that?" I had never heard this term used in relation to God.

He then began to explain that Jesus took my place for the punishment of my sins . I should have died on the cross for my own sins. I was the guilty one not Jesus. He said, "Rick if you will ask Jesus into your life and ask Him to forgive you of everything you have ever done –He will forgive you. He will wash away all your sins and will give you a new beginning, a new life." While he was telling me this, all the things I had ever done began to go across my mind. The more I realized how much I had sinned, the more I felt what Mark was telling me was too simple of a solution . I said,

"You mean all I have to do is ask Jesus to forgive me and all this goes away?" "Yes" He said to me. It sounded too easy. God had given Moses 613 laws and ceremonial laws so that man could learn how to live a holy and righteous life before God; and Mark was telling me it was just there for the asking. That I could be "saved" and spend eternity with God based not on what I did but based on what God did.

"21 For since, in the wisdom of God, the world through wisdom did not know God, it pleased God through the foolishness of the message preached to save those who believe.22 For Jews request a sign, and Greeks seek after wisdom;23 but we preach Christ crucified, to the Jews a stumbling block and to the Greeks foolishness,24 but to those who are called, both Jews and Greeks, Christ the power of God and the wisdom of God.25 Because the foolishness of God is wiser than men, and the weakness of God is stronger than men." 1 Corinthians 1:20-25

I left that night and headed home. As I was walking I looked up at the sky and saw all those beautiful stars. The palm trees blowing in the gentle breezes. I began to feel that same presence that I felt on the beach in Maui. All of a sudden I said "Jesus if you are really real, please forgive me of all my sins and come into my life." Immediately I felt like a big load I had been carrying came off of me. I actually felt a physical change take place. Jesus saved me. I felt completely different. I didn't understand all that happened but my life was different. The following days proved a major change had taken place in my life. Everything around me looked more beautiful. I asked my mother one night if I could help her wash the dishes. She was shocked. "What has gotten into my Ricky?" My little sister and I would fight all the time and all of a sudden I felt such love and compassion towards her. I began to treat her nice. She was shocked. After a week

I realized that I had stopped cussing. I didn't even think about or even have the desire to smoke pakalolo anymore.

You did What?

Finally one day my parents asked me what had happened to me that I was acting different. I told them "I asked Jesus into my heart" They became very upset with me. "We are Jewish, we don't believe in Jesus!" But that didn't matter to me. I knew my life was changed. My parents decided to send me to a counselor in our school to convince me I was just following a fad. Then my Grandfather wrote me a letter to try to convince me I was wrong in my beliefs. Then more letters started to come. I received several from my Grandpa's Rabbi and then I received a threatening letter from the Jewish Anti-Defamation League. No matter how many people tried to convince me that I was wrong, I knew my life had changed for the good.

Many Jewish people have a hard time seeing Jesus as the Messiah. Much persecution has come to the Jews in the name of Christ. There were the crusades in the middle ages where many Jews were killed. Some Jews even believe that Hitler was a Christian. My Grandfather was called a "Christ Killer" by many Catholic employees that worked for him. Is it any wonder why so many Jewish people won't even take the time to look into the fact that Yeshua is the true Messiah they have been looking for? The many atrocities that have taken place over the centuries since the time of Jesus has driven many Jews far from Christianity. They don't realize that just because someone calls themselves a Christian does not mean that they are a true representation of Christ. Jesus preached love, He walked love. When a person receives Yeshua (Jesus) in their life they are transformed. They take on His character.

" Therefore, if anyone is in Christ, he is a new creation; old things have passed away; behold, all things have become new." 2 Corinthians 5:17

Called and never turning back

Mark invited me to go to a church youth camp and even paid my way. It was on the north shore of Oahu in Mokulea. While I was there God did a mighty work in my life. During the morning prayer time I heard people speaking in tongues. This is a prayer language that God supernaturally gives His children when they are filled with the Holy Spirit. I had read about this gift in the Bible but I had not experienced it yet. I was hungry for more of God so I asked for prayer to receive what is called "The Baptism in The Holy Spirit". At each service I went forward to the front while people prayed over me to receive this blessing. But nothing happened. I became very discouraged. I wondered if there was something wrong with me. I went back to the room and was feeling sorry for myself. Then God spoke to me and said "Did I not teach you to praise me in every situation?" I knew that was the right thing to do so I began to praise Him and as soon as I did the discouragement lifted from me. The next morning I went forward again for prayer more determined than ever. But nothing happened yet again. Suddenly the minister was standing in front of me and said "Take your eyes off of tongues and put them on Jesus" I didn't realize I was focusing so much on the gift that I wasn't focusing on the giver of the gift. Immediately I had a vision and I saw Jesus seated on a throne and I was baptized in the Holy Spirit. I began to laugh and speak in tongues. The power and the presence of God was so strong that I felt as though my body was going to explode.

9

" You will show me the path of life; In Your presence is fullness of joy; At Your right hand are pleasures forevermore." Psalm 16:11

The minister speaking at the youth camp prophesied over me and told me of the calling God had placed on my life. I knew in my heart it was true. I knew God had called me into the ministry. The next day I was baptized in the ocean and experienced God's presence again in a beautiful way.   When I returned home from the camp I was on fire and zealous. My brother whose name is also Mark shared a room with me. I said "Mark, blink your eyes" He blinked his eyes. Then I snapped my fingers and said "Jesus is coming back soon and just like that, I am going to be taken and you are going to be left behind if you don't ask Jesus into your heart." Then I went to sleep. Little did I know that he stayed awake all night watching me because he thought I was going to disappear. That night Mark was scared into to accepting Jesus Christ into his life, which later on became a close walk with the Lord. Today Mark is a minister in Hawaii and making a difference in many people's lives. One by one the people in my family began to experience the life changing touch of Yeshua Ha Mashiach (Jesus The Messiah) my sisters, my mother and then my Grandparents who had fought me so hard trying to convince me how wrong I was. They opened   their heart to the   Messiah and were saved. Hallelujah!!

Chapter 2

Genuine or Counterfeit?

"Beloved, do not believe every spirit, but test the spirits, whether they are of God; because many false prophets have gone out into the world." 1 John 4:1

Not everything that is supernatural is God. Many people think just because they have a supernatural experience that it came from God. I learned an important lesson early on in my walk with the Lord. One day I was eating chili and rice at Zippy's in Kaimuki, Hawaii. I saw a man bow his head and pray. I heard a voice say to me "That man is a Christian" The voice was supernatural. I knew I heard it and I knew it just wasn't me drawing a conclusion. I went over to the man and said "Praise The Lord, are you a Christian?" He said "I belong to the Universalist Unitarian Church. We believe all religions lead to God." Then he told me that the seven spirits of God mentioned in Revelations in the Bible represented the seven major religions of the world. The more he talked, the more I became confused. I knew deep inside what he was telling me was wrong, but the voice I heard said he was a Christian. So I asked God "Why would you tell me that this man was a Christian when obviously he was not?" God answered me and told me that the voice I heard was not Him and that not every supernatural voice I hear is God speaking to me.

"But the Helper, the Holy Spirit, whom the Father will send in My name, He will teach you all things, and bring to your remembrance all things that I said to you". John 14:26

"However, when He, the Spirit of truth, has come, He will guide you into all truth; for He will not speak on His own authority, but whatever He hears He will speak; and He will tell you things to come.14 He will glorify Me, for He will take of what is Mine and declare it to you". John 16:13-14

The Holy Spirit leads us into all truth and we to need learn to know the voice of God above all other voices. **God's voice will never contradict His written word in the Bible.** If what you are hearing does not line up with the Word of God as written in the Bible then you can be sure it isn't God. We need to test the spirits whether they are of God. The Bible is a safety net for true believers to keep them from getting deceived.When looking to the written Word of God you can run into another problem. There are many people who interpret what is written from their own perspective or experience or they try to fit their experience to an isolated scripture to prove their experience is from God . This is a dangerous problem and leads to deception. Remember when Jesus was tempted in the wilderness by the devil and the devil used scripture to try and deceive Him? But Jesus having the full understanding of the Word of God and a balanced view of it, was able to combat the deception with the scripture using it in its right context.

Be diligent to present yourself approved to God, a worker who does not need to be ashamed, rightly dividing the word of truth. 2 Timothy 2:15

Now you have done it!

About two months after I had given my life to Christ I was kneeling in prayer. I had been learning the importance of seeking God in the morning and preparing my heart for the day. All of a sudden curse words towards God filled my thoughts. I was horrified and shocked. Then a voice spoke to me and said "Now you have done it, You have blasphemed the Holy Spirit and it can not be forgiven you." I had read the scripture that said:

"Therefore I say to you, every sin and blasphemy will be forgiven men, but the blasphemy against the Spirit will not be forgiven men.32 Anyone who speaks a word against the Son of Man, it will be forgiven him; but whoever speaks against the Holy Spirit, it will not be forgiven him, either in this age or in the age to come. Matthew 12:31-32

Condemnation filled my heart. I felt hopeless and felt like I had committed the unpardonable sin. Then the Holy Spirit began to minister to me and reveal that the whole experience was an attack and an attempt of the devil to try to deceive me and to separate me from the one who truly loved me unconditionally. The devil wanted to take advantage of my lack of foundation in the Word of God and tried to use The Word of God to deceive me. Thank God for 1 John 3:20-21 that says;

For if our heart condemns us, God is greater than our heart, and knows all things.21 Beloved, if our heart does not condemn us, we have confidence toward God.

The Holy Spirit ministered to me and showed me that the devil wanted to steal my confidence toward God. Since that experience I have been able to minister to others that have fallen prey to the same types of deceptions. I have known people who have cut off their own fingers or maimed a part of their body because of this type of deception based on the scripture that says:

"If your hand or foot causes you to sin, cut it off and cast it from you. It is better for you to enter into life lame or maimed, rather than having two hands or two feet, to be cast into the everlasting fire.9 And if your eye causes you to sin, pluck it out and cast it from you. It is better for you to enter into life with one eye, rather than having two eyes, to be cast into hell fire. Matthew 18:8-9

We must keep the Word of God in balance, understanding the full counsel of God. The greater foundation of God's Word in our lives, the less chance of deception entering our lives.

Into your presence?

One night I was lying on my bed in my dorm room in Bible College. I was hungry to experience God in His supernatural realm as I laid there I felt a presence come over me. I felt tingly all over And my spirit began to leave my body as I yielded to this presence. I thought God was bringing me up to heaven to experience heaven so I did not resist. But thank God for The Holy Spirit in us because all of a sudden I heard the Holy Spirit say to me "Can you praise me right now?" I realized I was bound and I could not praise Jesus. It took every bit of strength I could get to call out the name of Jesus. As soon I did the deceiving spirit let go of me and I was free. Since then I have had experiences from God of Him taking me up into His presence. But I have learned to be led by the Holy Spirit, because not every supernatural experience is from God.

Chapter 3

God Cares About The Little Things

6 "Are not five sparrows sold for two copper coins? And not one of them is forgotten before God. 7 But the very hairs of your head are all numbered. Do not fear therefore; you are of more value than many sparrows. Luke 12:6,7

God cares about the little things. Some people think it is foolish to ask God what you should wear or if you should eat this or that. Making these type of decisions should come out of common sense. God gave us a brain didn't He? I agree with the fact that wisdom comes from God and that he has given us the ability to make decisions and also a free will to make choices. But what many people miss out on is the blessing of hearing God in the small things.

"For My thoughts are not your thoughts, Nor are your ways My ways," says the Lord "For as the heavens are higher than the earth, So are My ways higher than your ways, and My thoughts than your thoughts." Isaiah 55:8,9

Inconvenienced just for a Tract?

When I headed for Bible College in California from Hawaii, I was traveling with another student. She had 12 pieces of luggage and I had 2. Can you imagine two inexperienced travelers traveling with 14 pieces of luggage? When we were leaving at the airport one of my friends came up to me and said. "The Lord told me to give this to you" I thought for a moment he was going to hand me money but instead he handed me a Gospel tract that was written to minister to Jehovah Witnesses. I was a little disappointed and said thanks and slipped into my Bible. When we landed in San Francisco I called the Bible college and said "Hi we are two students from Hawaii and we are enrolled for this semester. We are at the San Francisco airport please come pick us up" They told me that they don't pick up students but if we took a bus to Santa Cruz they would find someone to get us.

I started asking around "How do I catch a bus to Santa Cruz?" I was told that I would have to catch a Greyhound bus from downtown San Francisco but with all our luggage there was no Greyhound bus that could handle our luggage going to downtown. So we had to catch an Airporter bus to downtown and then go six blocks to the Greyhound station to catch our bus. I had no concept of six blocks in San Francisco. We had to pay porters every step of the way to help us with our luggage. We finally got to downtown and found that the Greyhound station was too far for us to take our luggage so we needed a taxi. The taxi driver looked at our bags and us and began cussing. He threw our luggage every way he could into the car and then cussed some more as he drove crazy for six blocks. We were so scared . We arrived at the Greyhound station and I ran to the window and said " I need two tickets to Santa Cruz." The woman behind the counter said "I'm sorry young man but that bus left 20 minutes ago and there are no more for today." I said "What can I do?" She said "Well ....You could take a bus to San Jose and then transfer to a Peerless Stages bus to Santa Cruz." So that is that we did .

Finally we were on our way. We were relaxing from the stress of the whole ordeal and then we heard the driver announce "Next stop San Francisco Airport." What? The San Francisco Airport? That's where we had started ! God why would you do this to us? We have come to serve you and to prepare for the ministry ,why? I was so confused. The bus started heading for San Jose. As I sat there wondering why my day was going the way it had I began to hear a conversation take place in the seats directly behind me. A man was sharing the Gospel with a young man. I began to pray for him. As I listened more the Christian man was ministering to a Jehovah Witness. The man said I wish I had a Bible with me to show you these things. I grabbed my Bible and held it above my head and handed it over the seat to the man. He said "Praise God!" He opened the Bible and there was the Gospel tract about Jehovah Witnesses. As he shared from this tract he led this young man to Christ. Now I knew why I was so delayed and inconvenienced. But that was not all. When we transferred to the Peerless Stages bus the driver was a Christian. We shared where we were going and he told us about his church in Santa Cruz. This church was the church my friend ended up attending.

When we got to Santa Cruz it was very late. I called the college and thank God someone answered. They said there was no one to pick us up but there was a resident assistant meeting going on in the dorms so they asked if anyone would like to pick up two students from Hawaii. Mike, one of the resident assistants, said he would. He came to get us in a Ford Mustang. That was an experience getting all that luggage in the car. I was exhausted only to find out that we were a day early and that we could not stay in the dorms. We had to go sleep in the gym on cots. Suddenly Mike said "Do you have a roommate?" I said "No, was I suppose to arrange that?' He said "Yes, well why don't you be my roommate. And because I am a Resident Assistant I am already in the dorm and you can move in tonight." Mike ended up being a great roommate. God's delays are not His denials. The next time you are delayed and it doesn't make sense, trust that God is at work and he has a plan. God had a plan from the smallest detail of speaking to someone to give me a Gospel tract before I even left on my journey. Lord ,You are so awesome! You are amazing!

Why do I need two Pens?

One day after classes had started at the college I was rushing to get to class. I was going to be late so I was quickly gathering my things to hurry out the door. When God said "Bring two pens, someone is going to need a pen in class" I stopped for a moment and grabbed another pen. I got to my class and while I was sitting down the person in front of me was frustrated and trying to get his pen to work. He turned around and said "Do you have another pen? Mine just ran out of ink" I said "I sure do" and with a smile handed my other pen to him. Now this may seem like a small matter but as I began to think about it , I started realizing how big God really is. Think about it. He knew ahead of time that the pen would run out of ink. He cared so much about that small need that he stopped me in my tracks to make sure that need would be met. That young man may have received a pen from God that day, but I received an understanding that God really does care about every detail of our lives. That thought has comforted and carried me through many situations in life.

"O LORD, You have searched me and known me. 2 You know my sitting down and my rising up; You understand my thought afar off. 3 You comprehend my path and my lying down, And are acquainted with all my ways.4 For there is not a word on my tongue, But behold, O LORD, You know it altogether. 5 You have hedged me behind and before, And laid Your hand upon me. 6 Such knowledge is too wonderful for me; It is high, I cannot attain it." Psalm 139:1-6

Chapter 4

Dreams & Visions

"And it shall come to pass in the last days, says God, That I will pour out of My Spirit on all flesh; Your sons and your daughters shall prophesy, Your young men shall see visions, Your old men shall dream dreams". Acts 2:17

Many times God has spoken to me through a vision or a dream. At age 18 I was working in a warehouse pulling tires and packing trailers for delivery. It was hard work. I worked 12 hours a day. I would come in when it was dark and leave when it was dark. I only weighed about 140 lbs and the people I worked with were older than me and much stronger. I wanted to share my faith with them but felt a little intimidated. Every day I would try to live my testimony in front of them but I was afraid to speak up. One night I had a dream. It was so vivid I actually thought I had woke up and it was happening. In the dream I heard a noise and jumped up and looked out the window of my room into my neighbor's yard. I could see the front door of their house. I saw a thief trying to break into the house while they were sleeping. Then I heard God's voice say "Warn the people that a thief is trying to break into their house." But I was afraid, I couldn't say anything. Then He said "If you cannot warn the people at least scare the thief away." I couldn't do that either. I was paralyzed with fear. Then I woke up and realized I was just dreaming. I didn't understand the dream until the next day while I was working and God opened my eyes to the fact that the devil was trying to break into the lives of the people I was working with and they didn't even realize it. He had placed me there for a reason. I needed to speak up. God had given me the responsibility to pray for them and to tell them about Jesus. He also wanted me to pray against the works of darkness that was trying to break into their lives. I began to speak up and share my faith with them. They were all very receptive. Many of them came to church with me and were saved. When I was leaving that job to go to Bible College, I was told that the first day I was hired everyone agreed that I wouldn't last a week there. But I worked hard and lived my walk with God in front of them. I had earned their respect. I was so glad that God helped me through that dream to get beyond my fears and insecurities and share the Gospel.

A Grandstand Christian

Therefore we also, since we are surrounded by so great a cloud of witnesses, let us lay aside every weight, and the sin which so easily ensnares us, and let us run with endurance the race that is set before us Hebrews 12:1

I was lying on my bed in my dorm room in Bible College praying. I fell asleep and had a dream that I was in a big stadium. I was sitting on the third level near the top of the stadium. I looked and saw that I was all dressed up to run a race. I had running clothes on and also special running shoes.

I also noticed I was muscular and in shape. Then I noticed my shoes were untied. While I was bending down to tie my shoes I heard a gun go off. Immediately I thought "I am suppose to be in this race." So I ran down the third level, the second level, the first level with every ounce of strength I had I ran onto the field. No matter how hard I was running I was way behind everyone else . I could not catch up. Then I woke up. Hebrews 12:1 immediately filled my thoughts. While I thought on this dream and the scripture , God convicted me in my heart that I was being a grandstand Christian. That He had equipped me with everything I needed to run the race but I was observing and not participating. Then He pointed out that just a simple thing like having your shoe untied can keep you out of a race and cause you to stumble. That "sin that so easily ensnares us" I layed there thinking about the little things that so easily ensnare me but I needed to get to the source of the problem. Then I fell asleep again and God gave me another dream.

Too Busy to Eat

"Your word I have hidden in my heart, That I might not sin against You". Psalm 119:11

I was standing in front of a huge buffet. There were all kinds of food. All my favorites and more. I began to pile my plate high with all these awesome foods. Just when I was about to put something in my mouth I was caught away and found myself busy doing something. I wasn't doing anything wrong, I was just busy. In the middle of what I was doing I remembered all the foods awaiting me. I started to head towards the buffet and I was caught up somewhere else doing something. This happened several times and I never made it back to that delicious outlay of foods. Then I woke up. God showed me that He had given me His Word for me to read every day. A buffet of good things to eat to strengthen me daily and give me the necessary things I need spiritually to be strong and healthy. But I was using the excuse of being too busy to take time out to read the Bible and to fill my heart with His Word. Then I realized that this was the root to my problem. That day I tied my shoes and began eating. I get dressed everyday and I eat

Cruise Ship Vision

Visions are similar to dreams but you are awake and not sleeping. There is a difference between day dreaming and having a vision. Some people let their imaginations take them all over the place. But when God gives you a vision it is not your imagination but instead it is a message from God to you and for others. I was standing worshipping during a service one day and I had a vision. I was on a cruise ship. I walked by pools of refreshing water where people were laying out in the sun and relaxing. I entered into the dining room where people were enjoying the most amazing outlay of food. I left the dining room and went to the edge of the ship to look out over the ocean. To my surprise I saw an ocean of sewage and thousands of people crying out for help. I saw one person go under and come up and then go under again never to be seen again. I felt an urgency that I needed to do something to rescue the people from this ocean of sewage. I ran to the pools of refreshing water and cried "Come with me- there are people who our dying. They need our help. Hurry grab a life preserver" . No one would move, so I ran into the dining room and said the same thing. But no one would come and join me. After pleading with the people about 14 decided to join me. We grabbed the life preservers and threw them into the ocean. We began to rescue people and pull them up into the ship. Now we had another problem. They were covered with sewage and they smelled bad. The only way I could get them to the showers was to take them past the pools of refreshing water and through the dining room. As I took them the people relaxing by the pools began to complain. "Get them out of here they are ruining our time relaxation." Then I brought them through the dining room. People began to get mad. "Why are you bringing them in here you are making us lose our appetite. You are ruining our meal. Then the vision was over. I knew God was showing me a picture of the church. Some churches have become like a cruise ship. A place catered to making life entertaining, refreshing and full of resources to meet our every desire. I know that God does provide all these things and more for us. But many have forgotten the lost world out there. Many people are crying out for help. They are sinking in the ocean of sin that covers our world like sewage. But who is willing to step away from their own needs and care for the needs of others? To take the time to help someone out of their life threatening problems. Many times when people come into a church they still have problems that they need to work through. They need to get cleaned up and we need to have patience with people as we walk them through to victory. I don't ever want to lose the burden for the lost. I have found that I have fallen into the cruise ship mentality at times. This vision has helped me to keep what really is important at the forefront of my thinking.

"Do you not say, 'Four months more and then the harvest'? I tell you, open your eyes and look at the fields! They are ripe for harvest." John 4:35

I was kneeling in prayer inside our church sanctuary. I saw another vision. In the middle of the sanctuary was a huge shiny red combine. A combine is a harvesting machine. I saw people standing around the combine and polishing it. I looked closely at the machine and realized some things that didn't seem right. The machine was unused. It was new. Everyone was so proud of it as they continued to polish it over and over again. Also it was in the middle of the sanctuary instead of outside in the harvest fields. God asked me "What is wrong with this picture?" Then He showed me that many churches have built a very impressive ministry. A ministry that they are very proud of. They spend all their time polishing their ministries wanting a perfectly functioning machine. But they don't take it out to the harvest fields. They just continue to polish things week after week while the fields are ripe for harvest. My prayer is that Christians everywhere would take their "impressive ministries" and get out into the harvest fields and reach the lost. The church is like a bath tub. If you can get fish in the tub it is pretty easy to catch them. But if you are really going to catch fish you need launch out in the deep and go fishing.

Chapter 5

You want me to give what?

"Give, and it will be given to you: good measure, pressed down, shaken together, and running over will be put into your bosom. For with the same measure that you use, it will be measured back to you." Luke 6:38

While I was in Bible College, money was scarce; but I did manage to scrape up enough to buy a very used classical guitar—$10—and taught myself to play. I spent the summer after high school working twelve-hour days to earn money for college. But just before classes started in the fall, I gave it all to my father to help the rest of the family survive a financial crisis. Through God's grace, my freshman year was made possible with a grant and a student loan.

Once at Bible College I formed a Christian music group with fellow students. While I got by with my old guitar, I needed a better guitar to minister for the Lord. From time to time, I even mentioned this desire in my prayers. The following spring, I was blessed with a tax refund of $273. The first thing I did with that money was buy a Takamine acoustic guitar with a hard case. I then had a custom leather strap made and embossed with the word "Alleluia."

I loved my new guitar and started using it in my ministry right away. While in prayer one night, I heard the Lord speak to me very clearly saying, "If I asked you to give your guitar away, would you do it?" I was surprised by this request and hesitated to answer. A few minutes later, I heard Him again, "If I asked you to give your guitar away, would you do it?" This time, I resolved in my heart that I would do whatever God asked. Although I didn't understand why He wanted me to give away the very thing I used for His glory, I answered, "Yes Lord; if You ask, I will give it away." I heard nothing else that evening and finally concluded that He was just testing my heart and my motives.

The next day, I put my guitar in the trunk of the car and headed off to school. While I waited for a friend to come out of the dorm, the Lord spoke very clearly to me again. This time He said, "I want you to give your guitar away." My heart started pounding and I nervously asked, "To who, Lord? Who?" I closed my eyes and instantly saw a face. I recognized him immediately. It was a young man I had seen from time to time on campus. But I didn't know his name nor did I know how to get in contact with him. Without hesitation, I said, "Lord, I'm going to drive through the campus one time. If I see this guy, I'll give it to him." As we pulled out of the driveway, to my surprise the very first person I saw was him jogging past the car. I said "stop the car!" and yelled, "Hey you, come here." As he came up to the car somewhat out of breath, I asked, "Do you have a guitar?" He looked at me confused and said "I do, but last night it got broke in half."I leaped out of the car and said "Follow me; I've got something to show you." I opened the trunk, popped the clasps on the case, and showed him my Takamine. "Wow; that's beautiful!" he exclaimed. "It's yours." I said. Consider it a gift from the Lord. He was shocked and overwhelmed. All of a sudden, I noticed the leather strap with "Alleluia" stamped down the middle.

Aware that it was one-of-a-kind, and feeling that giving up the guitar was already a considerable sacrifice, I asked, "Do you have a strap on your old guitar?" "Nope," he replied. Again, the Lord prompted, "Give it to him." And so I did.

Now I was faced with a new dilemma. Our group had three services scheduled that week; and I didn't know how we were going to meet the commitments without my guitar. Not to worry; God knows all and sees all. Almost immediately, those three ministry invitations were canceled. Naturally, I wondered what the Lord was up to; but at that point it was the end of the semester and I was going back to Hawaii.

At home, my brother had gotten away from the Lord and slipped into drugs. I had prayed for quite a while that he would turn his life around when I received the news that he and a drug buddy had recommitted their lives to Christ. As I got off the plane in Honolulu, my brother and his friend met me. While we walked to the parking lot, his friend asked if I owned a guitar. "Not anymore," I replied, "I just gave mine away." His eyes got big and he said that the Lord had been dealing with him about giving his guitar to me. Naturally, I assumed it would be old and beat up; but to my surprise, it was a Takamine made of rosewood with its own hard case. This guitar was four times the value of the one I had given away. I was overwhelmed by God's love and goodness toward me.

The next day, one of my old friends from church asked if he could borrow my guitar. "Sure," I said, "it's the Lord's guitar." A couple days later he returned it. When I opened the case, I was shocked to see a beautiful hand-painted leather strap attached to the guitar. It had been embossed with the word "Alleluia." I immediately called my friend and said, "Hey, man, you forgot your strap." "No, I didn't," he said, "The Lord told me to have this made for you. Be blessed, my brother!" I have learned that you can never out give the Lord. We must learn to hold everything that He blesses us with, with an open hand to Him. He should always have the right and the authority in our lives to decide what we should do with our property, money, talents and more. I trust Him. He knows what He is doing. It is always exciting to see what He does with the seeds that He asks us to plant for Him.

" Now may He who supplies seed to the sower, and bread for food, supply and multiply the seed you have sown and increase the fruits of your righteousness" 2 Corinthians 9:10

Chapter 6

The Best Counselor

"I will instruct you and teach you in the way you should go; I will counsel you and watch over you." Psalm 32:8 NIV

I have discovered that The Holy Spirit is our best counselor. There are many good counselors in this world and God uses them to counsel us. In fact accountability to others and receiving wisdom from trained professionals can really help. But there are times when we are faced with issues in our lives that we need a supernatural encounter with The Counselor, The Holy Spirit. I have always been a person that is small in physical stature. Participating in certain sports like football or basketball when you are short is not an easy task. Many things in life were a constant reminder of how short I really was. I didn't realize how it produced insecurity in my life. I wanted people to accept me and like me.

My first semester in Bible College I had two friends from Hawaii. We felt comfortable with each other because our common ground of being from Hawaii. I wanted to impress these guys and show them how cool I was and also how spiritual I was. The more I tried the more I became what some would call a "clingy" friend. They began to avoid me. I didn't understand what was happening. One night my roommate Mike said "Let's go to church, I invited two girls to go with us, we can take my Mustang and then afterwards go and get ice cream." It sounded like a great date. I wanted to make a good impression on these girls. Maybe one would like me, who knows, maybe I would find a girl I liked.

When we arrived at church something started happening to me I didn't understand. I felt all alone in this big church. As the service continued I began to feel like I was going to burst out in tears and cry. By the end of the service I couldn't take it anymore. I rushed out of the church and began to cry and couldn't stop. Mike and the two girls finally found me. He asked "Rick, what's wrong?" I cried "I don't know, I don't know what's happening to me. Please take me back to the college." We got in the car, everyone was so quiet and I was crying. Mike decided to put on some music. The words to the song were "Picking up the pieces of my life, bringing new releases just in time…" as it continued to play I cried even harder. When we finally reached the campus I said "Drop me off at the Chapel." As soon as I got inside the chapel I fell to my knees and cried out "God, what's wrong with me?" I thought in my mind that I was going to have to spend all night in prayer trying to figure out what was happening to me. Immediately I heard Him say "You don't love yourself" I did not expect that response. I stopped crying and knelt there surprised by the information I had just received. Then He began to run across my thoughts all the times I acted insecure, wanting people to accept me, wanting people to like me. The more He brought those thoughts across my mind, the more I realized how much I really didn't love myself. At first I felt hopeless and I blurted out "You're right, I don't love myself, I don't know how to love myself." He said "You're right, you don't know how to love yourself, but I am going to give you the ability to love yourself." Right then He filled me with a love that removed the insecurities out of my life. From that point forward I began to be a friend to others, a friend people wanted to be around. I began to accept myself for who I am and who God made and called me to be. Today I forget that I am a short person. I feel like a giant inside. I'm still not the greatest football or basketball player, but it doesn't matter to me anymore. I am who God made me to be.

Throw the Rock into The Ocean

God has healed me from so many things in my life. I was invited to the Island of Maui to minister to the students and counselors at Teen Challenge. I was just a little over one year old in the Lord. I was growing quickly and God was using me to minister to many people. One afternoon I decided to take a walk on the beach. I walked along the extensive sand praying, singing and having the best time with the Lord. I came upon a beach that had many black lava rocks and the ocean looked black because of all the lava rocks. I heard God say to me " Pick up one of those rocks and throw it into the ocean." That seemed like a strange request, but I knew I was hearing Him clearly so I did it. I threw as hard as I could and saw it land somewhere far off to my right. Then I heard Him say "Now go and find it!" "What? Find it? – Lord that would be almost impossible, there are so many rocks in there, and even if I got close to the location, how would I know I found the right rock?" His reply surprised me. He said "Then why do you keep trying to dig up your old sins? I have buried your sins in the depths of the sea and have put a no fishing sign over them." I didn't realize I had been digging up the failures of my past but I had felt a lack of confidence in my walk with the Lord because of it. That day I learned that God had really forgiven me. I don't have to allow the past to dictate how I feel about my relationship with God. I can walk with confidence that He is for me and not against me. That He is the cheerleader in my corner. That He wants me to succeed more that I want to succeed.

" For if our heart condemns us, God is greater than our heart, and knows all things. Beloved, if our heart does not condemn us, we have confidence toward God." 1 John 3:20,21

Chapter 7

Ask Jesus First

We could avoid so many problems if we would just learn to ask Jesus first. That was the motto of our singing group. We had a piece of paper taped on the dashboard of the car written in bold letters "ASK JESUS FIRST" Whenever we didn't know our next step, we always asked Him first. He taught us how to hear His voice as we traveled by faith across the United States. We had a few engagements set up but a lot of space in between to fill. With just a car and a little bit of money we listened everyday for direction and the most amazing things would happen.

We had finished ministering at a church in Rifle, Colorado and we had two weeks until we were suppose to minister in a church in Kansas City, Missouri. We had no place to go. We thanked the pastor in Rifle and took off. About a mile down the road we stopped and prayed and waited until we received instruction from the Lord. All of us heard that we were suppose to go to a town in southwest Colorado called Durango. Logically this did not make sense because first Durango was the opposite direction from Kansas City and we had limited funds for gas and food. Also we had never been to Durango and we didn't know anyone there. We started heading there anyways because we all knew we had heard from God. When we got halfway there we stopped the car, got out of the car and found a quiet spot by ourselves and prayed again. We needed to know more. When we all got back to the car we compared what God had spoken to us and we all received the same thing. We heard that we were going to minister in a service that night in Durango. That didn't make sense to us because we rarely heard of a church having a Thursday night service. Most churches had midweek services on Wednesdays. When we got closer to Durango we stopped in Silver Springs. I went to a phone booth and looked through the yellow pages for a church that advertised Thursday night services. I didn't see any. All of a sudden a Christian bookstore listing seemed to jump off the page at me. God was magnifying this listing and said to me. "I want you to go to this bookstore and you will receive further directions when you get there." I noted the address and got back in the car. I told everyone to take me to the address God had directed me to. They all asked me what was there but I just told them to take me there and they would see.

When we arrived at the store we went inside. We started looking around at the products and wondering what would happen next. I heard a shout come from behind the counter. The man behind the counter started shouting "Praise God, Praise God." We all went over to see what was going on. One of the members of our group had told the man behind the counter who we were and about our singing group. The man said "When I got up this morning I heard the Lord tell me to put a big pot of Gumbo on the stove, I am sending you a singing group, I want you to feed them and have them minister in the Bible study at the store this evening." Well here we were, hungry and excited and amazed at the leading of the Lord! That night we ministered at the Bible study and afterwards they took an offering to help us financially and they also asked us if we could minister the next night at another Bible study. We did and many people were touched by God. The finances that came in were enough to carry us for the next two weeks until we arrived at our next engagement.

The Mansion on The River

"I will instruct you and teach you in the way you should go; I will guide you with My eye." Psalm 32:8

Our singing group was traveling on our way to Charlotte, North Carolina. It was Friday night and we had made it to the southern tip of Illinois. We knew we needed to get to Nashville, Tennessee because we had some money sent to us in the mail to the general delivery. Being tired we pulled into a camp ground and slept outside under the trees. About 4 AM it began to pour heavy rain. Running to the car we all jumped in. We all stared at each other, tired, wet and wondering what to do next. Little did we know God had an eventful day planned for us. We needed to get on the road. It didn't make sense to sit there so we headed out. About 6 AM because of detours we got lost off the main highway and we were going down a country road in Kentucky. All of a sudden we saw a car in front of us crash into a tree. We got out and ran to the car. A lady was bleeding and in a daze, the steering wheel was bent and she was pinned in. One of us ran to a nearby house and had them call emergency. The police arrived and was able to help her. If we had not been there she may have not received the help she needed. The policeman looked at my license and saw it was from Hawaii. He was amazed that someone from Hawaii was on this back road in Kentucky at 6 A.M. But God knows what He is doing. We all concluded that this was the reason He got us up so early and on the road. But there was more. We finally reached the main post office in Nashville, Tennessee at 12:15 PM. When we went inside we discovered because it was Saturday that the post office had closed at 12 P.M. What were we suppose to do? How would we get our money? We couldn't stay there two days until Monday and our itinerary was not going to bring us back that way. I heard some noise behind the postmaster's door. I began to knock and knock. Finally a postal service clerk answered the door and said "We are closed." I explained our dilemma and the clerk decided to help us. A few minutes later we had the letter with the money in our hands. We saw another reason God got us up so early. But there was more.

When we left Nashville everyone in the group heard God tell them that we were going to stay in Knoxville, Tennessee that night and that He was going to lead us. When we reached Knoxville we were all led to take the 2nd exit. We were hungry and were going to get something to eat. Instead of going to a restaurant we all agreed to go to the grocery store. I was jumping out of the car when the Holy Spirit said "Stop! I don't want you to go in there. I want you to get your Bible and lean against the car and begin to read it." This was hard for me because I didn't want to miss out on anything. Plus I wanted to pick out what I wanted to eat. But God had different plans. I was leaning against the car and a young man that was gathering the carts saw me. He said "Praise God, are you a Christian?" I smiled and said "Yes, I am." I began to tell him about our singing group thinking that this would lead to our next step. But he just said "Great, well I need to get back to work." I thought, Lord that was nice but what are we suppose to do next? Then I heard the Holy Spirit say " I brought that young man to you to assure you that you are hearing my voice. Keep leaning against the car and read your Bible." So that's just what I did.

About 5 minutes later a young man was walking past the car and saw it had California license plates. "Wow! You are a long way from home," he said. Then he saw my Bible and said "Are you a Christian?" I said with a smile "Yes, I am." As I shared about our singing group he got excited. Then he asked "Do you have a place to stay tonight?" I said "No" He got even more excited. He said "Our church owns a 22 room mansion on the river. Would you like to stay there tonight?" Right then the group came out of the store. We were so blessed by the offer. When we got to the mansion it was gorgeous and very elegant. The young man asked if we could minister to their youth group and then their young adult group the next night. We had the most wonderful time with them and we ministered to many young people. Was it worth it getting up at 4 AM that morning in the rain? It sure was. God's timing on things are not always our timing but after everything is over we can look back and see the wisdom of the way he took us.

Chapter 8

Open my Eyes

"And Elisha prayed, and said, "LORD, I pray, open his eyes that he may see." Then the LORD opened the eyes of the young man, and he saw. And behold, the mountain was full of horses and chariots of fire all around Elisha." 2 Kings 6:17

It is always amazing to have God open your eyes to something that was right in front of you but you never saw it. Like the time when the two men walked on the road with Jesus to Emmaus after His resurrection, but did not know it was Him. They sensed something but did not see who He was until later when they broke bread together and their eyes were opened. I had such an experience when God opened my eyes to the woman I was to marry.

Dottie and I had been traveling in a music group across the United States ministering wherever the Lord would open the door. We were on our third journey. Originally our group was eight people but now there were three guys and Dottie. We were in North Carolina and she got upset with all three of us. She said "I have had enough of you guys I am walking back to California." She stormed out of the place. We all looked at each other and my friend Jay said "You better go after her- I'll pray" So I chased after and stopped her. I said "Dottie why are you so upset?" She said "Frankly you guys treat me like I'm your mother, I'm tired of it." "I don't feel that way " I replied. "Well how do you feel?" she said. At that point I had the biggest revelation. God tore the scales off my eyes and told me "The reason you are fighting so much with her is because you are resisting the fact that you are in love with her." I slowly said out of my mouth "I think I am in love with you." I was stunned but knew it was true. Then she revealed that she was in love with me also. God was speaking so clearly to us that within ten minutes we both heard God tell us that we were to get married in 5 months on January 21 in Hawaii.

We went from no romantic involvement, no dating to being engaged to be married all because of what God revealed to us by opening our eyes. God confirmed everything that night. As Dottie and I entered the place we were staying we saw Jay on his knees praying. He got up with a stunned look on his face. He said "Is it true? Are you two getting married?" We looked at each other and smiled and said "Yes it is true." We were all in shock but we needed to hurry because we were working as counselors on the phone at the PTL Club in Charlotte during the overnight shift. We were not on camera because the show was airing at different times and they needed counselors to be available when people called. I was sitting next to Dottie taking calls. On the show they asked for Pastors to call in for prayer for their churches. Dottie received a call from a pastor in Hamilton,Ontario Canada. She prayed for him and then he said "Can I pray for you?" When he finished praying he said. "Do you see the young man sitting next to you? Everything is going to work out between both of you" Dottie thanked him and then she took the next call. It was a woman pastor from Kentucky. Dottie prayed for her church and then the pastor said "Can I pray for you?" Dottie said "Yes" the pastor began to pray "Oh Lord I pray that you will give this woman a Man of God! Huh? You have given her a Man of God! Oh Lord I pray that you will fill him with the Holy Ghost! Huh? You have filled him with the Holy Ghost!" Dottie began to say to the Lord "O.K. Lord enough, I get the picture." God had confirmed several times that what we heard was Him and that He had a plan. I told Dottie that I knew we were now engaged but I knew we were headed close to Niagara Falls so I told her let's make it official there. When we got to Niagara Falls it was night time. Dottie's favorite color is pink. I got down on my knees and said "Dottie will you marry me?" She said "Yes" and the lights on the falls turned pink. We were married on January 21, 1978 in Hawaii just like God said.

Chapter 9

Participating in Answered Prayer

12 "What do you think? If a man has a hundred sheep, and one of them goes astray, does he not leave the ninety-nine and go to the mountains to seek the one that is straying? 13 And if he should find it, assuredly, I say to you, he rejoices more over that sheep than over the ninety-nine that did not go astray. 14 Even so it is not the will of your Father who is in heaven that one of these little ones should perish. Matthew 18:12-14

Dottie and I had a friend in Bible College her name was Renette. She was from Las Vegas. She was a sweet young lady and she loved the Lord. Sometimes she would go through struggles and we would minister to her and as time went on we all became very close. The school year ended and we all went our ways for the summer. When school started up in September, Renette did not return. We didn't know what happened to her. Our hearts were always burdened in prayer for her and we kept asking the Lord to touch her and if there was any possible way for us to get in contact with her again. When January came the Lord put it on our hearts to have our singing group travel across the United States ministering wherever He would open the doors. Our first stop was Price, Utah where our piano player was from.

We ministered in her church and then headed to Los Angeles where we were going to sing at the wedding of a friend. On the way to Los Angeles we saw the highway sign that said "Las Vegas next 14 exits" Immediately we thought of Renette. As we prayed, the Lord spoke to us and said "Tonight you will minister in Las Vegas." I remember whispering a prayer. "Lord if there is any way show us how to get in contact with Renette." As we began to pray for direction the Lord began to speak to us. We heard "Take the next exit. turn right, turn left" As we were driving being led by the Holy Spirit, He led us right in front of a rescue mission. We got out of the car and went up to the door and knocked. As we introduced ourselves the Pastor who answered the door shouted "Praise God" He said that the group that was supposed to come and minister in the service that was starting in 45 minutes called and canceled and he had no one to minister.

We ended up preaching, singing and leading several people to the Lord that night. After the service was over the Pastor said "Do you want to come see our church?" We said "Sure" He led us all the way across to the other side of Las Vegas to a huge church. As we walked into the church the Choir was practicing. Looking across the vast sanctuary our eyes saw a familiar face. It was Renette. We ran to her and embraced her. After the practice Renette confessed to us that she was away from the Lord but still went to Choir practice to keep her mother off her back. That night we prayed with her and she recommitted her life to Christ. She invited us to stay in her house that night. The next morning as we were having a prayer time and devotional she joined us and began to cry. As we shared The Lord revealed to all of us that she was suppose to be traveling with us. Her mother agreed that she should go. But there were two problems. Her father and her job. Her father was not a believer and would not understand and she had just started a great job. She spoke to her father and to her surprise he said "I think this would be the best thing for you." Her boss at her job told her the same thing. They said she would have a job waiting when she returned. So Renette packed up and away we went together down the road. God had answered our prayers and he used us to see it through.

" *Also I heard the voice of the Lord, saying: "Whom shall I send, And who will go for Us?" Then I said, "Here am I! Send me." Isaiah 6:8*

There have been many times when God has allowed me to be part of seeing my prayers answered. He is always looking for people who are yielded and available. Many times He will use you to be a participator to the answer to your prayers in times and in ways you never expected.

Preparing the way

One night I was at a prayer meeting in Grand Junction, Colorado. The presence of God was manifesting very strongly as I was overwhelmed in intercessory prayer. As I was praying in the Spirit I had a vision, I saw a man sitting on the side of a mountain on an Indian reservation in Arizona. I could see his form but I did not recognize him. He had been fasting and praying to God for direction for his ministry. I prayed intensely over him and knew in my heart God was going to give him the answers he needed. Then the burden lifted. Shortly after this prayer experience God called Dottie and I to move back to Hawaii. My family was living on Maui at the time so we went there. I thought God would open a ministry opportunity there, but God had a different plan. After a month in Maui and lots of prayer nothing was opening up for us. The Lord said "I want you to go to Kauai" I thought , "Where would I go?" Then I remembered a friend Robb from Bible College was now a pastor in Kapaa so I decided to call him. I thought maybe God would open up a Youth Pastor position at Robb's church. I called him and told him I was sensing the leading of the Lord to come to Kauai. He replied "Why don't you come for a visit and let's see what God has."

As I stepped off the plane I felt like I was home. Kauai is beautiful and Pastor Robb had a great church. I thought this is perfect for Dottie and I. While I was there Pastor Robb said "Rick there is a church in Kekaha that does not have a pastor. They need people to speak every Sunday. Are you available to speak this Sunday night?" I replied that I was. Then the Lord said to me "You are going to be the pastor of that church." I said "How can that be? I am 24 years old." I thought about that scripture that said you should not put a novice in a place of authority. But God had plans. The next day in Sunday school the message was about Josiah who became king when he was 8 years old. That blew my theory. God kept speaking to me. "You are going to be the pastor of that church." Then I thought –"What if they don't want me? I can't make them want me." I had found out that the pastor who founded the church had been there 25 years. Why would an established church want a novice as a pastor?

"Let no one despise your youth, but be an example to the believers in word, in conduct, in love, in spirit, in faith, in purity." 1 Timothy 4:12

It was a 45 minute drive to the church. During the drive the Lord kept speaking to me. By the time I arrived at the church I was fully convinced I was going to be the new pastor. I stood at the door greeting people like I was the pastor, it just came naturally. God blessed the preaching and ministry that night and the head deacon came up to me after the service and said "I have been speaking to the people and the other deacons and that they all agree, Will you be our pastor?" I agreed because God had already spoken to me about it.

Dottie and I moved to Kauai and began our ministry in Kekaha. God blessed that church as we saw many people get saved and the church began to grow. One day a Pastor Allen moved to a town nearby Hanapepe with his family and started a new church there. We became friends and we began to work together. We were talking one day and the most amazing story unfolded. He said that he had been a pastor on an Indian Reservation in Arizona and he had been on a 40 day fast praying for direction for his ministry. One night he was sitting on the side of a mountain earnestly seeking God and God revealed to him that he was to go to Kauai in Hawaii and pastor a church there. So the next day he called to Hawaii and found out that there was a church in Kekaha that needed a pastor. He knew immediately he was supposed to be the pastor. But he needed to make a lot of preparation to move to Hawaii and things took longer than expected. By the time he was able to make the move he found that the church had already found a pastor. He knew God had called him there so he decided to start a church in a neighboring town. After he shared this story I told him about the vision I had in Grand Junction , Colorado. When we compared notes it was the same day he was on the mountain side. Then God spoke to me and said. "I sent you here to prepare the way for Pastor Allen to be the pastor in Kekaha." without hesitation I told Pastor Allen. "You are suppose to be the pastor in Kekaha." He was surprised that I would so easily give up my position to allow him to step in. But God had made it so clear he had sent me as a forerunner. I shared the story with the church and they understood my heart and embraced Pastor Allen and his family as their new pastor.

One in a Million

7" Where can I go from Your Spirit? Or where can I flee from Your presence? 8 If I ascend into heaven, You are there; If I make my bed in hell, behold, You are there. 9 If I take the wings of the morning, And dwell in the uttermost parts of the sea, 10 Even there Your hand shall lead me, And Your right hand shall hold me". Psalm 139:7-10

The Lord opened another position for me on Kauai to work with a church in Lihue as an Assistant Pastor. I also became the Teen Challenge Director on the island . I would go into the Kauai Correctional Facility every week and minister to 40 inmates. I did this for two years and led several of them to the Lord. When they got out of jail I would take them down to the ocean and baptize them in water. There was a pro basketball player from Brazil named Carlos in jail. He had been caught with cocaine and was incarcerated there. He gave his life to the Lord in one of our meetings. Later when he was released the warden told him he needed to leave Hawaii or possibly face another prison sentence because there was an outstanding warrant for him in Honolulu on the island of Oahu. As soon as Carlos was freed I took him down to the ocean and baptized him in water and then took him to the airport. I told him to keep in contact with me but I didn't hear from him again. I would think about him often and pray for him. A couple years later I moved to Northern California and worked with a church in San Jose. One night we were headed to San Francisco for a large prayer meeting. As we were driving the Lord put it on our hearts to stop and catch B.A.R.T (Bay Area Rapid Transit), I had never been on a B.A.R.T. train and it was a sudden decision. We all felt very impressed to go into San Francisco this way instead of driving there. As we were traveling on the train I saw a tall man walking through the cabin. As he got closer I realized it was Carlos. Our eyes met and he shouted "Pastor Rick" and we hugged . I said "Carlos where have you been? What are you doing?" As we shared I discovered he had walked away from the Lord and was not going to any church. That night I ministered to him and he gave his life back to the Lord. We had a Brazilian pastor on staff at our church in San Jose so I got him in contact with Carlos. The pastor found him a church in San Francisco and Carlos became very involved. Later Carlos called to tell me that God called him to minister in the Azores Islands. He was sent out by his church. Out of all the millions of people on this planet, God saw to it that I would run into a man I had lifted up in prayer for two years.

Chapter 10

Saved from Death

".....He Himself likewise shared in the same, that through death He might destroy him who had the power of death, that is, the devil,15 and release those who through fear of death were all their lifetime subject to bondage." Hebrews 2:14,15

Being threatened by death can be a scary thing. Listening to the voice of God can keep you from experiencing a premature death or incurring injury to yourself. When I was pastoring in Kekaha, Kauai , I asked my friend Duane who I had led to Lord in high school to join my staff as the Youth Pastor. Both of us were young in the Lord but we were hungry for the things of God and wanted to touch lives in a way that would build and advance God's Kingdom. One day I received a call from a member in our church. She was crying as she asked me if I could come to the hospital. Her uncle had been pronounced dead by the doctor and the family needed the prayers and encouragement of their pastor. I asked Duane to come with me. As we entered the Kauai Veterans Memorial Hospital in Waimea we discovered the family standing around the bed of their dead uncle crying. I asked the Lord what I should do and He told me to begin singing the song- He is Lord – *"He is Lord, He is Lord He has risen from the dead and He is Lord, every knee shall bow, every tongue confess that Jesus Christ is Lord."* As I was singing this song the Holy Spirit said to me "Rebuke death and command life into this body." I got really nervous and just kept singing. Again the Holy Spirit said : "Rebuke death and command life into this body" I knew I was hearing God but needed some support so I turned to Duane "Do you know what the Lord just told me to do? He told me to rebuke death and command life into this body" Duane's eyes got real big and he said "The Lord told me to do the same thing." I said "Well if the Lord told you to do it and He told me to do it, we better do it." So I turned with confidence and looked at the dead man laying there in the hospital bed and boldly proclaimed " I rebuke death and command life into this body in the Name of Jesus Christ" Immediately the man's eyes popped open and he was alive. Everyone became excited as they witnessed a miracle right before their eyes.

I'm not lying, I'm a Christian

And the Lord will deliver me from every evil work and preserve me for His heavenly kingdom. To Him be glory forever and ever. Amen! 2 Timothy 4:18

I have been saved from injury and death by listening to the voice of God. While I was a student in Bible college I was working as an attendant in a Shell gas station in East San Jose , California. One night I was working by myself. I had the responsibility of closing the station. We had a cash box out by the pumps and a safe inside in the floor. Whenever cash levels would get high in the cash box , I would take the larger bills inside and slide them down a chute in the floor that went into the safe but didn't have the combination to open the safe. 15 minutes before I was to close the gas station, I went inside to take inventory of the oils I had sold. While counting the oils two men in trench coats approached me. As I turned to ask them if I could help them one grabbed me from behind and held a knife to my throat. He threw me to the floor and started banging my head against the cement. He was on top of my back as he held the knife close to my throat. He was screaming "Open the safe or I will kill you!" I responded "I don't know how to open the safe!" He began yelling "you're lying, you're lying" and kept demanding that I open the safe. The other man grabbed my keys and blurted out "I'm going to get my gun" As he left to go out to the cash register the man on top of me kept screaming "Open the safe or I'll will slit your throat." I shouted back at him and said "Listen – I'm not lying – I'm a Christian and I don't lie. – If you look at the safe it has a chute that I drop money down, I don't have access to the safe." He kept shouting "you're lying , you're lying." Because he wouldn't listen to me I began to speak in tongues out loud. As I began to speak he seemed to lose control as he shouted "Hey man what you doing – shut up – shut up." But I just kept speaking in the power of the Holy Spirit. As I was speaking the presence of God filled me and I heard the voice of God say to me "This man does not have it in the power of his hand to take your life. Your life is in My hands" And then I received a word of knowledge about the man on top of me. The Lord said this man has an Aunt who has been praying for him to come to Jesus and he has been running from God. Knowing with full confidence now that this man could not kill me I boldly said "You have an auntie who is praying for you to come to Jesus and you have been running from God." He began to cry and said "How do you know that?" I began to pray for him that he would give his life to Jesus. Then I said "Satan I bind you and I command you to get out of this gas station." Suddenly the man jumped up and ran out of the gas station. God had saved my life. I believe one day I will see this man in heaven. Listening to the voice of the Holy Spirit will always make a big difference in saving your life. It can be a matter of seconds that could make a situation turn one way or the other. It is so important to learn how to hear God's voice and to act in faith upon the things He speaks to you.

One second could have killed us

I was traveling in Colorado headed for a prayer meeting one Saturday night. I was in the back seat of a Ford Bronco and my friends Tony and Rhonda were in the front seat. Rhonda was 8 months pregnant. We were headed from Rifle, Colorado to Grand Junction. The road has the Colorado river on one side and canyon walls on the other side. There is a double yellow line on the road because it is too dangerous to try and pass with all the curves and no place to go. I was playing my guitar in back and we were singing praises to God. We were coming to a blind curve in the road and a Chevy Blazer tried to pass us. As the car was passing us another car from the other direction was about to crash head on into the Chevy Blazer. So Tony trying to get out of the way turned the wheel abruptly and we started heading straight into the Colorado river. Tony abruptly turned the wheel back and we flipped over and over. I did not have my seat belt on. My guitar and I were all over the place in that car. We landed on our side in the middle of the highway. I was so disoriented and didn't know which way was up. Suddenly I heard God's voice , it almost sounded audible. It shook me from my disoriented state. He said "Get up right now and get them out of the car. Another car is coming around the corner and you will all be crushed. I went from not knowing where I was to jumping to my feet. I began to pull Rhonda out of the car as I yelled to Tony and said "Get out now – another car is coming and we are going to be crushed.." Tony pushed his way out of the car as I dragged Rhonda to the side. A Lincoln Continental came flying around the curve and hit our car. The Bronco flipped over on its head and was completely crush in. Tony, Rhonda and myself stood on the side of the road without a bruise, scratch or broken bone. It was a matter of a second that we got away from that vehicle. Rhonda was checked later and the baby was fine.

Supernatural Is Natural

Chapter 11

Learn to Wait on the Lord

" Wait on the LORD; Be of good courage, And He shall strengthen your heart; Wait, I say, on the LORD!" Psalm 27:14

I remember the first year I became a Christian in Hawaii. My family decided to move to Southern California to open up a business. I wanted to stay in Hawaii to finish my senior year of high school. The school I was attending was a college prep boarding school so my family made arrangements for me to live in the dorms. When Christmas time came around my dad bought me a ticket to fly to Southern California for the holiday. I had never traveled by myself before and it was a little scary for me. When we were 1 hour from landing in Los Angeles the pilot said over the loud speaker on the plane " Folks, Los Angeles is completely fogged in we are going to have to land in San Francisco." Up to that point I had never been to San Francisco, I didn't know anyone there. There were four planes diverted to that airport and the place was packed with people and chaos. I didn't know what to do so I just followed the crowd. I waited in line to get to the airline counter. When I reached the airline representative she looked at my ticket and said " I am putting you in the Holiday Inn for the night, Go claim your baggage downstairs and go to the middle meridian for pick up. In the morning we will get you on a plane to Los Angeles." I headed downstairs and realized , my sister sent a couple boxes of presents for my family. I could not handle the luggage and the boxes so I paid a porter to get it to the middle meridian. While I was waiting I met two ladies from Tulsa, Oklahoma and discovered they were Christians and very nice. They said they were put in the Executive Inn. As we were talking the Holiday Inn van came, opened the door and said "Sorry folks, The Holiday Inn is completely full. We cannot take any more people. I began to panic. What was I to do. I had all my luggage there, how was I going to get things changed. I asked the ladies. "Can you watch my luggage while I go I try to get a new voucher?" They said sure but if their bus came they would have to leave. I took off running. My heart racing. I got to the bottom of the escalator and I heard God say to me. "STOP! WAIT HERE" it almost sounded audible. He said "Wait here until I say go." It was so hard for me. I thought about my luggage, I thought about the fact that it took me 45 minutes just to get to the counter before. I didn't understand why God would stop me and make me wait when time was not on my side. Suddenly He said "Now ,GO." I ran up the escalator and began breaking through the long lines trying to get to the line I needed to wait in. To my surprise an agent from my airlines was breaking through the lines and we came face to face. I said "I was given this voucher to the Holiday Inn – But they are completely full" She took it out of my hands and wrote

"Executive Inn" and signed it. I turned around and ran back to the middle meridian. Just when I did the Executive Inn van drove up. I got in the van. When we got to the Hotel I helped the ladies with their luggage and then got my luggage. I ended up the last in the line at the counter. When I got to the counter the man said. " I am sorry young man, but we do not have any more rooms." I was stunned. I stood there not knowing what to do. I must have had a distressed look on my face because he looked at me and then said "Oh, why not, I am going to give you the bridal suite". When I got to the room , it was awesome. I don't know why I was so impressed that there were seven lamps in the room, but that impressed me. I ended up having the most beautiful time in the presence of the Lord in that bridal suite. I felt the love of God wrap around me like a warm embrace. The next day I headed for Los Angeles rested and filled with the love and presence of God. Listening to the voice of God and learning to wait on the Lord made all the difference in a situation that was beyond my ability or understanding to handle myself.

Waiting really pays

"In the morning, O LORD, you hear my voice; in the morning I lay my requests before you and wait in expectation. " Psalm 5:3 NIV

Not too long ago I was invited to minister in a conference in Guadalajara, Mexico. I needed to buy three roundtrip airline tickets from Philadelphia. It cost me $1,000.00. Two weeks before the conference the pastor that was organizing the event called me and said "We have to cancel the conference because of the swine flu" I said " That's O.K. – I will come anyway" But he said "Please don't come, the government here is not allowing any public meetings while this epidemic is spreading." I was disappointed but understood. I called up the airlines to see what I could do with the tickets. They told me that I had non-refundable tickets and if I cancel I will lose most of the money but could use the remaining amount towards travel in the future if I travel within the year. I was about to cancel because I knew we were not going and I wanted to at least have what I could salvage from the tickets. Right before I was about to cancel, I heard God say "Wait, do not cancel." I didn't understand it. I didn't want to lose the money but I have learned to listen and obey. So I said "Thank you for the information, I will keep our tickets for now." Almost two weeks had passed and I was wondering about the tickets. I still had peace but had no other direction but to wait. Two days before we were scheduled to travel the airlines called me and said. " We have to cancel your return flight from Guadalajara and we have no alternatives for that day. We can either schedule you for a different day or we can give you a full refund of your tickets. Which choice do you think I chose? You're right. I said "well.....I think I will take a full refund, cancel my tickets." They told me it would take 4-6 weeks for me to receive a refund but the full $1,000.00 was back in my bank the next day. Waiting on God is a good thing but some people take it to an extreme and they shrug responsibility or they end up in denial about a problem or situation that needs attention or action. I have learned to follow the leading of the Holy Spirit. Not to be hasty to make decisions out of our logic or emotions. Also not to ignore the things we need to take care of. Learning to hear

God's voice can become a natural part of your life. He will give you the ability to discern what is right and wrong.

Surprised by God

"If we are faithless, He remains faithful; He cannot deny Himself." 2 Timothy 2:13

There are times we don't know what to do. Sometimes we just don't have the resources to take care of a problem. When you don't know what to do, the best thing to do is to place it in God's hands and seek Him for direction. This may result in a period of waiting with no answers. I received a bill in the mail from the Internal Revenue Service. It was for over $1,200.00 . I didn't know what to do. I didn't have the money. Because I didn't have the resources to handle this and I wasn't clear on my options. I decided to wait. Now there is a difference between procrastination and waiting. Procrastination puts off what you should do now. Waiting involves trust that there is a right timing to move. I didn't know what to do and I hadn't discovered any viable alternatives. The only option I knew was to pay the debt or suffer the consequences. I knew that it just wouldn't go away, although I wish sometimes problems would just disappear. Three weeks later I received a notice from the IRS in the mail. It said that if I didn't pay what I owed that they would seek to put a lien on anything they could find and levy my taxes. The situation was getting progressively worse. I didn't see any evidence of God providing to pay this debt. I didn't get any specific instructions through prayer. I discovered that I could set up a payment plan with the IRS but it would not stop the penalties. The penalties would keep adding up until the debt was paid in full. I decided to call and set up the arrangements. I was dreading this but it looked like my only option. An angel must have answered the phone because God surprised me with something I didn't expect. The person on the other end looked into the matter and said "We are going to cancel this debt, you do not owe the IRS anything, we will send you a letter confirming this." I sat there surprised and speechless. All this time I was trying not to stress over the matter. I couldn't see possibilities beyond the present options. God many times because He loves us will supernaturally intervene in a situation even when we have failed to exercise our faith. Thank you Lord! You are so good.

Chapter 12

Get the Picture?

"33 And with many such parables He spoke the word to them as they were able to hear it.34 But without a parable He did not speak to them. And when they were alone, He explained all things to His disciples." Mark 4:33-34

Many times God has spoken to me through pictures. He shows me a picture in my mind and immediately I know it is Him showing me something. I liken these pictures to parables because they tell a story with spiritual application. These pictures can work alongside the gifts of the Holy Spirit. The Word of Knowledge as God reveals knowledge about a person or situation. The Word of Wisdom as God reveals wisdom how to apply the knowledge that has been revealed. The Discerning of spirits as God reveals the influence affecting a person or circumstance. These pictures are similar to having a vision but it is like seeing a picture in your thoughts. It is different from having a vivid imagination because when you see these pictures you know without a doubt that it is God speaking to you. When I am praying for someone or a situation, or when I am worshipping the Lord, many times I see pictures. There have been so many that I would not be able to share all of them.

I remember praying for a couple. As I prayed I saw a picture of a rooster chasing a hen. The rooster was nipping at the hen aggressively. The hen was intimidated, scared and wanted the rooster to stop. But the rooster would not stop. Immediately through the picture the Lord was showing me that the husband was constantly attacking his wife with his words and that the wife wanted him to stop. As I shared what I was seeing and the interpretation of what I was seeing the wife started to cry. The husband could see that he had been hurting her with his constant verbal attacks. He repented right there and asked his wife to forgive him.

Another time I was praying for a woman to be filled with the Holy Spirit. Nothing was happening. As I prayed I saw a green Buddha head. That was strange because I was at a tent meeting in a remote town in Utah. Many times we assume things by appearances. My experience being from Hawaii is that most people who are Buddhists are Asians. This woman had blonde hair and was not Asian. But I knew what I was seeing was from God. So I asked the woman about what I was seeing. She looked at me amazed as she shared with me that she was raised a Buddhist but had given her life to the Lord. I told her that she needed to renounce any connection to Buddhism . As soon as she renounced it she was filled with the Holy Spirit and began to speak in tongues.

I was attending a two week ministry training seminar on Praise & Worship at the University of The Nations , YWAM base in Kona Hawaii. Many well known singers and musicians were there teaching. It was a wonderful experience. We were in a time of worship and I saw a picture of a bird trying to sing but the bird's mouth was full of things it had gathered. Its mouth was bulging to the point it could not sing. Then I saw an old fashioned street lamp on a busy corner where there were many cars going through the intersection. The cars were able to pass unharmed because of the light the street lamp was shining. The revelation the Lord gave me was that the song bird was fearful that its needs were not going to be met that it kept trying to gather as much as possible, worried and concerned about the future. Because of this fear the bird could not sing the way it was created to sing. The street lamp on the busy corner was taken for granted. It had been shining its light for years keeping many from accidents. But not acknowledged for what it had accomplished. I knew there was someone there who felt this way. So I shared what I saw and a very well known singer spoke up and said that what I shared described what they were going through. That day God healed that persons heart and freed them up to minister in greater capacity.

Many times the Lord has spoken to me through pictures that have caused me to draw closer to Him and to grow in my walk with Him. I was praying one day and saw a picture of a painter with a pallet in his hand and a brush. He was trying to paint a rainbow and wanted to have the colors pure and untainted. He took the brush and cleaned it over and over again. The Lord spoke to me and said that I was like the painter. The colors were His truth and the brush was my heart. He said that He had called me to paint a true picture of the colors of His love to the nations. But if I was going to

67

paint a true picture of Him I needed to keep my heart clean. I needed to wash my heart in the water of His Word daily.

I pray that I have painted a pure picture of His love through this book to you. Hearing the voice of God and seeing the results of our obedience to Him is the most natural thing that could take place in a Child of God's life. Supernatural is natural for the Christian. Please join me on this adventure. A journey that takes you every day on the path of blessings. A journey that will take you to the finish line until He calls you and me home.

" Every good gift and every perfect gift is from above, and comes down from the Father of lights, with whom there is no variation or shadow of turning." James 1:17

"My sheep hear My voice, and I know them, and they follow Me." John 10:27

"For though by this time you ought to be teachers, you need someone to teach you again the first principles of the oracles of God; and you have come to need milk and not solid food.13 For everyone who partakes only of milk is unskilled in the word of righteousness, for he is a babe.14 But solid food belongs to those who are of full age, that is, those who by reason of use have their senses exercised to discern both good and evil." Hebrews 5:12-14

About The Author

Dr. Rick Kurnow

Rick was raised in a Jewish home. He went to Hebrew school and had his Bar Mitzvah. When he was 13 his family moved to Hawaii. At age 17 a Japanese friend pointed Him to his Messiah Yeshua (Jesus). Ricks life was radically changed when he invited Yeshua into his life. That was in 1974. He immediately knew he had a call on his life and entered Bethany Bible College in Santa Cruz, California. He received a Bachelor of Science degree as a ministerial major. Rick met his wife Dottie at Bible College and they were married in 1978. Together they have ministered in churches and traveled for over 33 years. Rick has been mightily used of God to impact many lives. The gifts of the Holy Spirit flow richly through his ministry. In 2005 Rick received a Doctor of Divinity from The School of Bible Theology Seminary and University in San Jacinto, California, Dr. Kurnow currently resides in Corona California where he Co-pastors with his wife Dottie, Gates of Praise Worship Center in Ontario, California. Also Rick and Dottie frequently speak and minister throughout the USA and Mexico through Kurnow Ministries International. You can find out more about their ministry at _www.Kurnow.org_

Dr's Rick & Dottie Kurnow

Rick is also a recording artist with the release of 3 music CD's recorded with his wife Dottie. His most recent CD is "Here Comes a Miracle." He is also the designer of the New Covenant Messianic Tallit Prayer Shawl. Thousands of these prayer shawls have touched lives all over the world. Dr. Kurnow's DVD teachings "The Biblical use of the Shofar", "The Biblical Use of The Tallit" and "Yeshua Revealed in the Passover" has been distributed all over the world and has been a blessing to many.

Rick & Dottie are the founders of Shofars From Afar, LLC a company that supports the economy of Israel by offering Jewish, Messianic and Christian products. These unique gifts can be found at *www.ShofarsFromAfar.com*

Made in the USA
Charleston, SC
17 February 2012